It's All God

Introducing a Simple Spiritual Practice
Based on a Very Simple Notion

To Elaine, my soul mate and wife of 42 years, and to our children and grandchildren.

This book describes meditative practices that can lead to unfamiliar states of consciousness, which can be stressful for some people. Be sure to check with your doctor to see if you are healthy enough to meditate.

The very simple notion is that:

It's all God

The simple spiritual practice is:

Just start noticing that

This practice is easy to do, but when sustained over time, it has a cumulative effect that can lead to very profound realizations. It starts first as a notion, then it becomes a world view, and then it becomes a way of life.

It derives its effectiveness from a wholesome spiritual attitude combined with a certain continuity of intent.

It does not require that you stop doing the things that you enjoy.

It does not require that you separate yourself from family or friends.

It does not require that you practice austerities or seclude yourself.

It does not require you to have a guru – life itself becomes your teacher.

It does not even require that you believe "It's All God." You can think of it as a perspective, or a hypothesis. Just try it on like a suit of clothes. If the suit fits, wear it.

Contents

The Eternal Now

You Live in Two Worlds

You may not realize it, but you live in two worlds. One life is within the dimension of time. Your other life is in the *eternal now*.

In the dimension of time there are many polarities – gain and loss, joy and sadness, good and bad, life and death, and so on.

In the eternal now, these polarities do not exist.

In the dimension of time, you exist as an ego-entity, a being, a personality, or a separated individuality.

In the eternal now you do not exactly exist as a person. It feels like, "I am, but there is no me."

In the eternal now, nothing is ever born and nothing ever dies. Everything is exactly as it is. No words can describe this.

You are familiar with your life within the dimension of time, but you may not yet be aware of how you also live in the eternal now.

This little book will show how you can begin to awaken your awareness of your second life in the eternal now, and how you can live from that perspective.

Eternal versus Everlasting

Have you ever wondered about the difference between everlasting life and eternal life?

Everlasting life means that you continue to live as an ego-entity after your physical death.

Eternal life is life outside of the dimension of time – it is not something that will happen in the future.

In the dimension of time, God created the world a long time ago. The relation of God to the world is that of creator and created. God is fundamentally different from His creations. God reigns over His creations and sets forth laws for them to follow.

In the eternal now, All is God. Nothing exists apart from God. From the formless void, to galaxies, suns, planets, angels, humans, animals, insects, plants, microbes, rocks, grains of sand – all this is

God. God's Love embraces all of creation equally. God does not punish or judge.

Union with God

Starting with a wholesome spiritual attitude, you can eventually go beyond the level of thoughts about God, and move toward experiencing God directly. In other words, you can go beyond the dimension of time, and meet God in the eternal now.

In the eternal now, you let go of the idea of a separate self, and open your heart to the experience of union with God.

The essence of heaven is union with God

The essence of suffering is separation from God

Creating is Becoming

The notion that It's All God leads naturally to a holistic view of creation.

When we are free from the dimension of time, we say that God *creates* the world rather than God *created* the world.

Since nothing exists apart from God, we see that God *creates* the world by *becoming* the world.

The universe is the body of God

God becomes conscious by manifesting as sentient beings

One possible analogy is the way that a good actor creates a character in a play. The actor *becomes* the character for the duration of the play.

Another analogy that might work for you is that of a sunbeam. A sunbeam might say that it *is* the sun, in the sense that the sun is its original source, and in a manner of speaking, the sun is its true identity. The sunbeam is the sun, but it is not *all* of the sun.

Similarly, you may feel that you *are* God, in the sense that God is your original source, and in a manner of speaking, God is your true identity. You are God, but you are not *all* of God.

Two-Thirds One-Third

As long as you have the gift of a physical body, you will be living with the polarities that come with the dimension of time. Even so, you may long to experience God directly in the eternal now.

A good working solution is to move toward living two-thirds in the eternal now and one-third in the dimension of time. That way you will have a strong spiritual base, and still be able to function in the conventional world.

Find Your Own Balance

Two-thirds one-third may not be the right ratio for you. It is just the one that works for me. For the last sixty years I have had a great fondness for transcendental experience. For me, touching into these realms has been immensely inspiring and life changing.

You may prefer a different ratio. Whatever you choose, know that it will be a gradual transition. You move slowly toward what you want to be and how you want to live. Don't expect to accomplish this all at once.

A Wholesome Spiritual Attitude

Do these three things to foster a wholesome spiritual attitude:

> Know that we are all in this together.
>
> Know that you already have it.
>
> Take small steps.

We Are All in This Together

You may regard that you are taking up this practice (starting to notice that it's all God) for personal reasons — as part of your overall spiritual path. That's fine, but as you progress in your understanding you may very well notice that other beings are coming along with you. You can think of it as a kind of basic research, with a goal to increase the total amount of spiritual awareness in the universe.

As part of your wholesome spiritual attitude, you can make a conscious decision that you want all sentient beings to benefit from the progress that you make. In Buddhism this is called Dedicating the Merit. It purifies your practice and opens your heart.

You Already Have It

Sometimes folks use other words when they refer to Union with God – enlightenment, spiritual awakening, or being lotus born, for example. Whatever words you use, be careful, because each of these terms has preconceived associations that you will eventually have to work your way free of.

For now, let's use the term enlightenment. Somewhere around fifty years ago I had a powerful realization to the effect that all human beings already had the seed of enlightenment within them – that eventual enlightenment is built into the very nature of what human life is.

Additionally, while helping run meditation-related workshops, I started to notice what folks said when they had bits of direct experience. A common thread was the feeling that "I have always known this – how could I have hidden this from myself all these years?"

Growth toward enlightenment is a natural thing.
The seed grows and the fruit ripens.

Knowing that the seed of enlightenment is already
there within you, take this attitude:

*Enlightenment is not
something you get*

*It is something
you relax into*

Take Small Steps

If you want a role model, consider an inch worm.
Inch your way toward what you want to be and
how you want to live.

In the mid 1960s I lived in Laguna Beach, California. On a lark, I bought a small trimaran sailboat, and I decided to sail it in the harbor at nearby Newport Beach. I also decided that it would be good to take some sailing lessons, so that I would be less likely to crash into the very expensive boats that were docked there.

The trimaran was only fourteen feet long, so I not only had to learn how to steer the boat and manage the sails, but also how to use my weight to balance the boat so that the wind would not blow it over. My instructor explained that I should always make only small adjustments to my course heading – any sudden large adjustment would cause the boat to capsize.

Well, I never became much of a sailor, but his advice stayed with me. Along my own spiritual path I take small steps. Progress is slow, but I have a continuity of intent that keeps me going.

I am pretty happy with what I've become, and now I am starting to learn how to live.

The Role of Kindness

Aldous Huxley and his wife Laura were two of the earliest and greatest contributors to the "human potential" movement that flourished in the 1960s and 1970s. Aldous, toward the end of his life, was asked by a reporter to leave some parting words for humanity. Aldous said simply, "Try to be a little kinder." I like the way he put it, "**Try** to be a **little** kinder."

The Dalai Lama put it even more succinctly, "My religion is kindness."

Mother Teresa once said, "With God there is nothing small." In context, she was explaining how simple acts of kindness create ripples that propagate out and affect the entire world.

I would go a little further and suggest that:

*Every act of kindness creates
a link between the dimension
of time and the eternal now*

In the dimension of time, it might on occasion
seem necessary to pass judgment, or even to
strongly oppose things that you consider
unwholesome. But always remember to take
yourself and your opinions with a grain of salt.

Be kind whenever you can.

"I am God"

The Supreme Identity

Alan Watts was a free-lance philosopher who specialized in interpreting Eastern Wisdom so that it made sense to readers in the West. One of his early works was a book titled *The Supreme Identity*. I read that book somewhere around 1960 and it changed my life in a profound way. Alan and I later became friends, and in 1962 I had the good fortune to be part of a small group that traveled with him to Japan, where we visited temples and monasteries, and met with zen masters, tea masters, and scholars whom Alan had not yet met, but who knew him through collaborating on some of his books. As we traveled, Alan explained the history and philosophy that connected with the places we went and the people we met.

The concept of The Supreme Identity comes from an ancient spiritual tradition known as vedanta (sometimes called advaita vedanta). Within vedanta there are two sanskrit words – Atman and Brahman.

Atman is your personal soul – if you go deep within yourself, beyond your personality to the very core of your being, that is Atman.

Brahman is God, the creator of all life and the universe – the fundamental source of everything.

The Supreme Identity states simply that Atman and Brahman are one and the same.

Little i and Big I

Spiritual teachers in the West often speak of "Little i" and "Big I." "Little i" is your personal self – the one you already know – the one who goes by your name. "Big I" is your divine self – ultimately recognizable as God.

At the heart of your divine self is a stillness more profound than creation itself. Out of that stillness comes light, and out of that light comes the phenomenal world as we know it.

Your spiritual goal is to integrate "Little i" and "Big I" – your personal self and your divine self, so that they live well together. This is a big job, but trust that your wholesome spiritual attitude, combined with your continuity of intent, will move you in the right direction.

I am God

The statement "I am God" is at once the most arrogant and the most humble thing that you could ever say.

At the arrogant end of the spectrum it can suggest that the realization of your divinity somehow makes you superior to the person who has not had that realization. In zen practice the first peek into one's essence is called kensho or satori. In the immediate aftermath of satori, students of zen sometimes become rather puffed up – full of themselves. If this happens, the zen master will quickly slap it down, calling it "the stink of zen."

At the humble end of the spectrum, it can feel too daunting – how can I ever live up to the task of being an emanation of God in this life? I feel God's love and I want to benefit others, but I have no idea how to live in the light of that.

Midway between these extremes is a sweet spot that has just the right mix of an existential self-esteem combined with an attitude of humility in which you acknowledge to yourself that learning to live right is going to take a while.

Try This Simple Meditation

Sit quietly and close your eyes. Enter the eternal now. Feel the presence of your divine self in your Heart. Now let your earthly self dissolve, and abide only in your divine self. Then come back out into the dimension of time and find your earthly self.

Do this for short periods of time at first. Then, as it becomes more natural, increase the amount of time you spend within. This will help move your sense of identity in the direction of your divine self, toward the ratio that you chose earlier.

"Others are God"

Remembering that in the eternal now, creating is becoming, we realize immediately that:

God lives in me as me

God lives in you as you

Namaste

The sanskrit word namaste (pronounced namas-te) can be translated as "God within me greets God within you." This simple notion can become the basis of how you might relate to other sentient beings. When you acknowledge that others are God, it is natural to feel respectful toward them. You can build on this feeling of respect to also feel warmth toward others, and to treat them with caring and kindness.

Enhance Your Casual Interactions

To begin practicing "Others are God" start by upgrading the way you relate to people who are not family or close friends – for example, folks in line at the super market, or clerks at the DMV. Especially, notice how you relate to people who are being difficult – short with each other or with you.

When, in your opinion, another person is behaving badly, create a feeling of warmth and tenderness within your own heart, then put your attention on the other. Refrain from forming any further opinion about that person. Just listen carefully and say nothing. Often this simple adjustment to your own state will cause an immediate change in the other person's mood and behavior – not always, but surprisingly often.

After you have tried this a few times, you can broaden your approach to include everyone. As you approach each other person, feel warmth and tenderness. Continue the practice until it becomes your normal way of relating.

"It's All God"

Now, having spent a little time practicing "I am God" and "Others are God," you are ready to practice "It's All God." This includes not just sentient beings, but the entire world of your experience.

Start with the notion "It's All God" and then intend to experience that directly. Open your mind and your heart to whatever might come up for you. Practice with your eyes open, and notice any change in the way things look and feel.

Do this practice a little bit each day. Over time, you may notice that things begin to look different. You may feel that some kind of veil has been lifted and that you are beginning to see things more clearly. The sense of separation between you and the things you perceive gradually falls away. Things such as mountains, trees, and plants may seem to be illuminated from within with a sort of heavenly light. You may begin to experience what I call *glory moments*.

Glory Moments

William Wordsworth was a poet who lived from 1770 to 1850. One of his poems is *Intimations of Immortality from Recollections of Early Childhood*. Folks have interpreted this poem in many ways, but for me it seems to say that sometime in his early childhood, Wordsworth had a spontaneous transcendental experience in which he saw everything around him radiating light from within. It also appears that although he remembered how precious that experience was, he also felt that he would never be able to get it back. He wrote, "Nothing can bring back the hour of splendor in the grass, of glory in the flower." He was really sad about that.

To my knowledge, Wordsworth did not practice any kind of meditative discipline, and so it is understandable that he felt that he would never be able to get that experience again.

I am beginning to have more of these glory moments as I continue to practice "It's All God." I cannot bring them up on demand, but they come often enough that they are beginning to feel natural. I think this will also be the case for you if you maintain your wholesome spiritual attitude, and persist with the practice.

These glory moments will show you that you are coming along – see them as milestones, not as a goal in themselves. Your goal is God Realization – letting God become real to you in this life.

The Tapestry of Life

There is something else that develops when we contemplate "It's All God" – an appreciation for the interconnectedness of events. There is something that synchronizes things that we can perceive so that they are not as separate as we would expect them to be. There are "higher symmetries" that cause certain things to happen more frequently than they would if they just happened at random. Sometimes this is called serendipity. I call it the *tapestry of life*.

Take a few moments to relax and let your awareness flow through all the disparate parts of your life, and notice all the things and beings that appear. Keep "It's All God" in the back of your mind and look for connections that you had not previously noticed.

Develop an Attitude of Equanimity

Equanimity means living in the world without creating too many judgments or preferences.

27

Don't be too fixed in your ideas as to what is holy and what is mundane. There is always a wider perspective. With God, everything is precious. Remember:

> *There is no fundamental difference between pearls and swine*

The operative word here is *fundamental*. In this context, fundamental means from God's perspective. God's love embraces everything just as it is.

Even so, our physical bodies locate us in space and time, and in the dimension of time there is a difference between right and wrong. Each of us needs to decide how best to act, speak, and think in this world.

A common thread runs through the words of the great spiritual teachers: love God and love each other. Most also recommend kindness as a way of life.

The pillars of this practice are similar: Notice that It's All God, and be kind whenever you can.

Attributes of a Mature Spiritual Being

If you have read this far, then perhaps the "It's All God" notion has already become a world view for you, and you are ready to turn your attention to making it a way of life. A mature spiritual being knows how to apply the fruits of enlightenment to ordinary life situations. In very general terms, you try to do what reduces the feeling of separateness and increases the feeling of union with all and everything. It's a gradual thing – you grow into it.

I've already discussed the role of kindness, which is paramount. To this I have added five more attributes that I think characterize a mature spiritual being. The list of six then becomes:

Kindness
Happiness
Generosity
Patience
Self-Discipline
Wisdom

Those of you who have been exposed to Mahayana Buddhism may recognize four of these to be part of the Six Paramitas, sometimes translated as Transcendental Virtues. Many great sages and scholars have discussed these, so there is not much to be added there.

My focus in this book is to show how these Attributes of a Mature Spiritual Being flow naturally and almost automatically from your wholesome spiritual attitude and your continuity of intent.

Make Your Own Version

The remainder of this book will include a hodgepodge of examples showing how you can develop these attributes and apply them in your own life. But I have no way of knowing what you have to deal with, so you will be able to write your own version, which will be better for you.

Happiness

Do these two things to foster happiness:

Notice your perennial happiness.

Do less of what makes you unhappy.

Notice Your Perennial Happiness

Between the ages of 28 and 73 I had intermittent problems with chronic back pain. One episode lasted about three years, and toward the end of that three year period I noticed that I was really pretty happy. I realized then that being in a lot of pain did not automatically require me to be unhappy about it. At first this surprised me, but as I looked deeper I saw quite clearly that there were two selves involved – a personal self that really wanted the pain to end, and a less personal self that was happy no matter what. In accordance with the "I am God" notion, I call that perennially happy self my *divine self.*

An analogy might be an ocean, where the surface can be alarmingly stormy, but a few hundred feet down it is quite peaceful. Now admittedly, the captain of a vessel caught in a perfect storm will not want to be told that the ocean is peaceful just a few hundred feet below.

Even so, the memory of that realization that I had when I was in all that pain still sustains me.

Whenever you can, take this attitude:

*My divine self is
inherently happy*

Do Less of What Makes You Unhappy

Ordinary life can bring all sorts of hardships and sorrows, even to the luckiest of us. Even so, we usually have a choice – we can accept these as part of the tapestry of life, or we can add to our suffering by responding in a way that actually makes things worse.

For example, if someone were to insult me, I could go on a sulk about it, dwelling for days about how unjust the criticism was. Alternatively, I could detach a little, asking whether it was in any way valid, or whether I was doing something to give the wrong impression to that other person.

Similarly, if I were to be in some kind of accident, I could be primarily interested in making sure everyone knew who was to blame for it. Alternatively, I could be solution oriented, and just think about how to resolve the situation in a way that would be best for everyone involved.

Chances are you can find many examples of times when you had the choice whether or not to make a situation worse through responding in an unconstructive way.

What About Doing More of What Makes You Happy

I did not include this in the list above, because I think there are too many situations where it just doesn't work.

For example, you might get a raise or a promotion at work, or you might get some new clothes or a new car. At first this might feel really good, but before long a process called hedonic adaptation will make you regard your new situation as the norm, and the happy feeling will not last. You might even fixate on what could give you the next boost, and how you don't have that, and actually make yourself unhappy.

Somewhere around year 2005 somebody told me a story about a friend who had previously worked for one of the major Wall Street investment banks as an IT specialist. The job paid a very good salary, plus generous yearly bonuses, but the work environment was very stressful. The friend had accumulated about two million dollars when he decided to quit working and instead to write a book – something he had always wanted to do. A coworker decided to stay with the investment bank, and the two happened to meet about ten years later. The coworker told the friend, "if you had stayed you would now have more than ten million dollars." The friend then said to the coworker, "yes, but I have something you will never have." Then the coworker asked "what's that?" The friend replied, "enough."

Chasing happiness can be counterproductive:

Doing more of what makes you happy does not necessarily make you more happy

Generosity

Being generous, even in small ways, helps you to feel that you have enough and some to spare. It can soften the idea that you need to have more.

Stewardship Versus Ownership

An idea that you may find useful is that you don't actually own things – that whatever you have in the way of wealth or talent is what you have been entrusted to manage during this lifetime. Taking this attitude might make it easier for you to cultivate generosity.

Ditch the Idea of Winning

Remembering that the first pillar of your wholesome spiritual attitude is to know that we are all in this together, it then becomes natural to think of mutual benefit rather than your individual benefit. Avoid the idea that you can benefit yourself at the expense of someone else.

Try to find a balance between doing what benefits you and doing what benefits others. I like this way of putting it:

I live for others, with myself as one of those others

Ways to be Generous

If you have accumulated a lot of "stuff" you can ease into being generous by starting to give away some of your stuff. This will keep you from having to store or protect it. Some of this stuff may be sellable, but it may actually feel better to give it away.

If you have enough money to live comfortably, you might try giving away some of your money.

Being generous with your time may be a better way for you.

If you are more able-bodied than some of your neighbors, try helping them with chores that are difficult for them to do on their own.

If you are a good listener, let other folks know that you are available any time that they have something they need to talk about, and that you will not judge them based on what they confide in you.

Patience

When you are dealing with a truly urgent matter, it is usually best to take action rather than waiting for the situation to resolve on its own.

However, most of a typical day is full of situations in which patience helps. By letting yourself be irritated by little inconveniences, you will usually just make yourself unhappy. An extreme example of impatience is to become angry at the problem, which can lead to serious consequences. For example, an impatient driver might resort to extreme tailgating , or frequent lane changes, putting everyone nearby in danger.

Fortunately, your wholesome spiritual attitude gives you some tools to lessen your impatience.

Equanimity Helps

Cultivating an attitude of equanimity tempers impatience automatically. You can simply enjoy an alternate state of awareness. For example, when you have to wait in line at a retail store, you can savor the experience of being in the moment, or you can practice "It's All God." You can also practice feeling love toward the people around you.

Expectation Plays a Role

We don't usually feel impatient when we don't see a rainbow, because most of the time we don't *expect* to see a rainbow. Similarly, we don't usually feel sad when the rainbow goes away, because we don't *expect* it to last very long. Generally, your day will flow better if you refrain from having rigid expectations as to what should happen next.

You can be a positive example

A few months ago I had to wait for my turn to get some blood drawn for a lab test. The woman in charge of managing the queue was substituting for the usual staff member. She was not familiar with the computer screens involved and so everything took just a little longer. When my turn came, she said "I'm sorry you had to wait." I replied, "That's OK – I don't mind." At that moment I felt a flash of emotion coming from the other side of the room. Someone had apparently found it startling that I actually did not mind having to wait.

Try being patient in public. It might actually help others to be more patient.

Self-Discipline

In the context of the "It's All God" practice, self-discipline means training your mind so that you can:

> Do more of what brings you into a feeling of oneness with creation.
>
> Do less of what increases your feeling of separation.

These two criteria are good starting points for developing a way of life that builds upon your wholesome spiritual attitude. Your continuity of intent will help you stay focused on this goal, so that you will gradually develop the required self-discipline.

Some approaches to self-discipline start with lists of things that one should do and things that one should not do. In practice, starting with a fixed set of rules may not be the best approach, especially if these rules are imported from another culture or another century.

For me it works better simply to notice how my thoughts, words, and actions increase or decrease the feeling of oneness. Then I can gradually modify how I think, speak, and act. Here are some examples of how to modify common mental habits.

Be Less Self-Serving

Many of us live in subcultures that program us to take advantage of each situation so as to come out ahead. When you notice the urge to do this, simply ask yourself whether that is the best way to foster oneness.

Be Slow to Anger

Anger is an instinctive response that seldom leads to right action. When you become angry, you lose your concentration and it becomes more difficult to find a solution to the problem at hand.

Let Go of Resentment

In the course of ordinary life, people will on occasion treat you unfairly or in some other way they will let you down. It is almost never helpful to carry resentment into the future. When you notice yourself feeling resentment, or even desiring revenge, just let it go. Challenges to your self-discipline can arise suddenly in the course of a typical day. Gradually learn to take control of your mind when it tries to do something that does not align with your spiritual goal.

Wisdom

If you have read this far, and if you maintain a continuity of intent to develop the first five of these attributes, then it won't be long before you notice that you are significantly kinder, happier, more generous, more patient, and that you have more mental and emotional self-discipline.

It is OK to feel good about the progress you have made. However, there will still be two ways in which your practice can be improved:

Go beyond your personal self

Become better at benefiting others

Going Beyond Your Personal Self

To go beyond your personal self, simply change your attitude.

Rather than considering these five attributes as part of your individual personality, think of them instead as attributes of eternity, and allow yourself to be an open channel for them. Kindness, for example, can just flow from the eternal now through your personal self into the dimension of time, like air flowing through a flute.

You don't have to work at this – just allow it.

As you begin to allow this flow, you will experience brief moments of touching into eternity. Even a momentary flash of it can begin a fundamental transformation. Somewhere in some zen book I read this sentence:

Over a blazing fire
a snowflake cannot survive

In this context, it means that a touch into eternity is more satisfying than anything your personal self might desire, and so at that moment your personal self disappears.

This may not make sense to you at this stage of your practice. Don't worry – just set it aside and continue developing the first five attributes. Then come back and read it again, perhaps a year from now.

Dimension of Time – A Closer Look

Earlier in this book I drew a distinction between the dimension of time and the eternal now. I invited you to familiarize with the eternal now and practice moving your awareness back and forth between your ordinary life – that progresses through time – and the eternal now, where time does not exist. I even suggested living two-thirds in the eternal now and one-third in the dimension of time. That was my way of introducing the idea of eternal now so that it would be easy to grasp.

Now I want to move to a more general way of looking at it. The notion of a personal self is generated and maintained by a physical body – located in time and space and serving as a focal point for sense experience. To most of us, it is very convincing. But it is not the whole story.

Albert Einstein, one of the world's great thinkers, expressed it this way:

> "A human being is a part of the whole called by us universe, a part limited in time and space. He experiences himself, his thoughts and feelings as something separated from the rest, a kind of optical delusion of his consciousness. This delusion is a kind of

prison for us, restricting us to our personal desires and to affection for a few persons nearest to us. Our task must be to free ourselves from this prison by widening our circle of compassion to embrace all living creatures and the whole of nature in its beauty."

Now you can generalize the idea of the dimension of time and simply regard it as the perspective from which you identify with your personal self. The idea of spending two-thirds of your "time" in the eternal now becomes letting two-thirds of your awareness abide in the eternal now and one-third of your awareness identify with your personal self.

As you proceed in your practice, you may notice that you feel less of a distinction between these two realms, as the eternal now begins to infuse its way into the world of common experience. The phenomenal world begins to feel warmer and more effulgent. The eternal now begins to feel more natural and less like an abstract concept.

The notion that "It's All God" actually makes it easier for you to feel at home in the eternal now. Here's a quote from the great Indian sage, Ramana Maharshi:

When your standpoint becomes that of wisdom, you will find the world to be God

Becoming Better At Benefiting Others

Earlier, – in the section on generosity – I introduced the idea that you don't actually own things – that whatever you have in the way of wealth or talent is what you have been entrusted to manage during this lifetime. Now I want to take the concept of stewardship a step further, to suggest that the primary purpose of your existence as a human being is the opportunity to benefit others. From this perspective, it is good to try to apply your intelligence to make your actions more beneficial.

For example, catering to a child's every whim may at first seem kind, but if it is carried too far, the child may become moody in an effort to invoke more kindness. It might be better to gently guide the child to manage negative emotions as they come up.

Similarly, giving children too many material possessions may deny them the opportunity to become more resourceful at working within limitations.

When being generous you can look for ways to leverage your generosity. For example, you may know a person who is naturally generous with his or her time, but not particularly good at earning or raising money. Funding a beneficial project might be a way to leverage your money to do more good than a simple donation for a person's individual benefit.

If a person you know normally works to benefit others, but has experienced a setback, such as a natural disaster or loss of a job, you might help that person in the near term, knowing that he or she is likely to "pay it forward" when things get back to normal.

These are just a few examples of how you might use your intelligence to increase the amount by which you can benefit others.

At first, you may need to take an analytical approach to your decisions – carefully thinking what might be the real result of each action. However, after you have seen enough examples of how things play out, you will be able to use your intuition, and not have to think so much.

Wisdom develops in its own good time, but you will recognize it by the way that it becomes effortless. Eternity will guide your actions, and your presence will enrich those around you.